# DK READERS

## Pre-level 1

Fishy Tales
Colorful Days

Garden Friends
Party Fun

## Level 1

A Day at Greenhill Farm
Truck Trouble
Tale of a Tadpole
Surprise Puppy!
Duckling Days
A Day at Seagull Beach
Whatever the Weather
Busy Buzzy Bee
Big Machines
Wild Baby Animals
A Bed for the Winter
Born to be a Butterfly
Dinosaur's Day
Feeding Time
Diving Dolphin

Rockets and Spaceships
My Cat's Secret
First Day at Gymnastics
A Trip to the Zoo
I Can Swim!
LEGO: Trouble at the Bridge
LEGO: Secret at Dolphin Bay
A Day in the Life of a Builder
A Day in the Life of a Dancer
A Day in the Life of a Firefighter
A Day in the Life of a Teacher
A Day in the Life of a Musician
A Day in the Life of a Doctor
A Day in the Life of a Police Officer
A Day in the Life of a TV Reporter

## Level 2

Dinosaur Dinners
Fire Fighter!
Bugs! Bugs! Bugs!
Slinky, Scaly Snakes!
Animal Hospital
The Little Ballerina
Munching, Crunching, Sniffing,
and Snooping
The Secret Life of Trees
Winking, Blinking, Wiggling,
and Waggling
Astronaut: Living in Space
Twisters!
Holiday! Celebration Days
around the World

The Story of Pocahontas
Horse Show
Survivors: The Night the Titanic
Sank
Eruption! The Story of Volcanoes
The Story of Columbus
Journey of a Humpback Whale
Amazing Buildings
Feathers, Flippers, and Feet
LEGO: Castle Under Attack
LEGO: Rocket Rescue
¡Insectos! en español
Gigantes de Hierra en español
Ice Skating Stars

# A Note to Parents

DK READERS is a compelling program for beginning readers, designed in conjunction with leading literacy experts, including Dr. Linda Gambrell, Director of the School of Education at Clemson University. Dr. Gambrell has served on the Board of Directors of the International Reading Association and as President of the National Reading Conference.

Beautiful illustrations and superb full-color photographs combine with engaging, easy-to-read stories to offer a fresh approach to each subject in the series. Each DK READER is guaranteed to capture a child's interest while developing his or her reading skills, general knowledge, and love of reading.

The four levels of DK READERS are aimed at different reading abilities, enabling you to choose the books that are exactly right for your child:

**Level 1** – Beginning to read
**Level 2** – Beginning to read alone
**Level 3** – Reading alone
**Level 4** – Proficient readers

The "normal" age at which a child begins to read can be anywhere from three to eight years old, so these levels are only a general guideline.

No matter which level you select, you can be sure that you are helping your child learn to read, then read to learn!

LONDON, NEW YORK, MUNICH,
MELBOURNE, and DELHI

**Project Editors** Anna Lofthouse
Naia Bray Moffatt
**Senior Art Editor** Cheryl Telfer
**Art Editor** Catherine Goldsmith
**U.S. Editor** Elizabeth Hester
**Production** Shivani Pandey
**DTP Designer** Almudena Diaz
**Jacket Designer** Dean Price
**Picture Researcher** Angela Anderson
**Photographer** Bill Ling

**Reading Consultant**
Linda Gambrell

First American Edition, 2003
05  10  9  8  7
Published in the United States by DK Publishing, Inc.
375 Hudson Street, New York, New York 10014

Published in Great Britain by Dorling Kindersley Limited

Library of Congress Cataloging-in-Publication Data
Wallace, Karen.
   A trip to the zoo. -- 1st American ed.
   p. cm. -- (Dorling Kindersley readers)
   Summary: Two brothers learn about wild animals by visiting the zoo.
   ISBN 0-7894-9219-9 (pbk.) -- ISBN 0-7894-9307-1 (hardcover)
   1. Zoo animals--Juvenile literature. [1.Zoo animals. 2.Zoos.] I. Title. II. Series.

QL77.5. W35 2003
636.088'9--dc21
                                        2002011688

Color reproduction by Colourscan, Singapore
Printed and bound in China by L Rex Printing Co., Ltd.

The publisher would like to thank the following for
their kind permission to reproduce their images:
Position key: c=center; b=bottom; l=left; r=right; t=top
   **Getty Images:** Vince Streano 8-9.
   **Masterfile UK:** Daryl Benson 25; Greg Stott 24.
   **Zefa Picture Library:** 11; 16-17.
   **Jarrold Publishing** at Woburn Safari,
   courtesy of the Marquess of Tavistock
and the Trustees of the Bedford Estates Park: 12–13c.
All other photographs taken at Woburn Safari Park, courtesy of the
Marquess of Tavistock and the Trustees of the Bedford Estates
   **Models:** Billy Ling, Matt Ling, Terrie Ling
   **Illustrations:** by Venice Shone

All other images © Dorling Kindersley
For further information see: www.dkimages.com

Discover more at

# www.dk.com

 **READERS**

BEGINNING
1
TO READ

# A Trip to the Zoo

Written by Karen Wallace

DK Publishing, Inc.

Billy was a boy
who loved wild animals.
He read books about them.
He watched movies about them.

During vacation, Billy's mom
had a surprise for him,
and his little brother, Matt.
It was a trip to the zoo.

Billy and Matt were so excited.
First, they saw a huge elephant.
She was having her
teeth checked.

Then the elephant
walked around slowly
to let the children pet her.
"Her skin feels so hairy,"
laughed Matt.

"Look at the rhinos," Billy said.
"Their horns look very sharp,"
  Matt replied.

horn

Billy told Matt that rhinos
may seem clumsy,
but they can run very fast.

"Look! Those horses have stripes,"
said Matt.
"Those aren't horses,"
said Billy.
"They're zebras."

"Can you ride a zebra?"
asked Matt.
"No, zebras are wild animals."

stripes

"Here are some more
striped animals," called Matt.
Billy looked at the tigers
lying under the tree.

They looked so peaceful.
It was hard for him to believe
that tigers are fierce hunters
in the wild.

"No stripes this time, Matt,"
Billy laughed.
"Giraffes have
big and small patches."

Matt was feeling hungry.
"I think the giraffes
are hungry, too!" said Billy.

patches

Next, they went to the ape house.
"Look–that gorilla is
taking care of her baby,"
said Matt.

It was time to go
to the sea lion show.
But Billy did not want to.
He was staring at the
gorilla's big nostrils!

nostril

The sea lion show was starting.
The sea lion came up and
touched a fish with his nose.

nose

Plop! Plop!

Then he gobbled the fish and dived back into the water.

Billy and Matt looked through the underground window at the pool.

They watched a sea lion use
his flippers to swim underwater.

flipper

After lunch, they went to see
the squirrel monkeys.
"Where are they?" asked Matt.
"Look up in the trees," said Mom.

They were running through the
branches, and one was hanging
upside down by its tail!

tail

"Look, those koalas are climbing trees, too," said Matt. "Their sharp claws help them to grip," Billy explained. "Hold on tight, baby koala!" called Matt.

claws

Some furry wallabies
hopped by.
"They are like kangaroos
but smaller," said Billy.
"Watch me jump
like a wallaby,"
said Matt.

Boing!
Boing!
Boing!

"I wish we could take
some animals home," said Billy.
"I'm afraid we can't do that,"
said Mom.

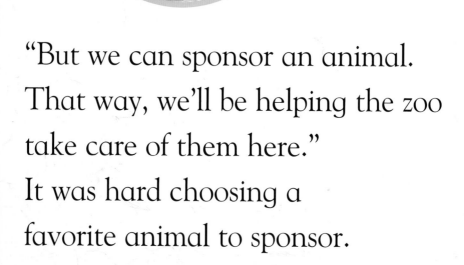

"But we can sponsor an animal.
That way, we'll be helping the zoo
take care of them here."
It was hard choosing a
favorite animal to sponsor.

29

When they got home,
Billy and Matt
started making
a thank-you surprise
for Mom.

They made paintings
of all the animals
they saw.
"Now," said Billy,
"we have a zoo
at home!"

31

# Picture word list

horn

page 8

nose

page 18

stripes

page 10

flipper

page 21

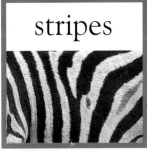
patches

page 15

tail

page 23

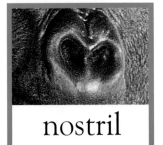
nostril

page 16

claws

page 25

32